T0262732

NATIONAL GEOGRAPHIC
KiDS

5-Minute Dinosaur Stories

Moira Donohue

NATIONAL GEOGRAPHIC
WASHINGTON, D.C.

Contents

Growing Up Dinosaur

The forest is dim and humid. Leafy ferns carpet the ground. It's some 77 million years ago—a time when dinosaurs rule Earth. One dinosaur, a female *Maiasaura* (my-ah-SORE-ah), plods through the forest on four legs. She snips a leaf off a shrub with her beak.

FERNS
were on
EARTH before
DINOSAURS.

This *Maiasaura* is ready to lay eggs. She digs in the ground to make a large, bowl-shaped nest. Then she piles dirt around the outside rim of the hole. She looks around. Nearby, other *Maiasaura* females are making their own nests. They nest in groups.

Scientists believe **MAIASAURA** returned to the **SAME NEST** year after year to lay eggs.

A MODEL NEST AT A MUSEUM

The *Maiasaura* lines the nest with leaves and weeds. Then she lays her eggs. There are 30 of them! The eggs are about six inches (15 cm) long—the size of an ostrich egg. The eggshells are hard.

Not all dinosaur eggs were hard like *Maiasaura* eggs. *Protoceratops* (PRO-toh-SER-ah-tops) eggs were leathery, like a sea turtle's. Not all dinosaur eggs looked the same, either. Some were green or tan. Some were blue, like a robin's egg. Some dinosaurs laid long, thin eggs. *Maiasaura* laid eggs shaped like ovals.

SEA TURTLE EGGS

BEIBEILONG (BAY-bay-long) laid **EGGS** that were **18 INCHES** (45 cm) **LONG**.

Keeping the eggs warm will help them hatch. But *Maiasaura* is too big to sit on her eggs. If she did, she would crush them. She has another way of keeping the eggs warm. The leaves she lined the nest with will rot, giving off heat as they decay.

What's inside the eggs? The *Maiasaura* has to wait a long time to find out. Chicken eggs hatch baby chicks in about 21 days. But dinosaur eggs took much longer—sometimes several months! The mother dinosaur waits and watches.

Finally, *crack!* The babies break through the eggs! Tiny *Maiasaura* dinosaurs pop out.

The babies are about 20 inches (51 cm) long— the size of a cat. Some dinosaur babies can walk and find food for themselves right away. But *Maiasaura* babies are helpless at birth, like human babies. They need to be fed. The *Maiasaura* mother finds leaves and brings them to her babies for dinner.

The *Maiasaura* babies grow quickly. By the time they are eight years old, they will be 30 feet (9 m) long. That's about as long as two cars!

MAIASAURA

T. REX needed **20 YEARS** to grow to its **FULL LENGTH** of **40 FEET (12 m).**

Maiasaura babies live in family groups called herds. To stay safe, they keep close to adult dinosaurs. One day, when they are all grown up, the *Maiasaura* will make nests and raise baby dinosaurs of their own.

Today, in Montana, U.S.A., you can see where some *Maiasaura* nests were. Scientists discovered fossilized eggs and bones in an area now called Egg Mountain. Because of this site, we know a lot about how *Maiasaura* lived.

FOSSILIZED *MAIASAURA* EGGS

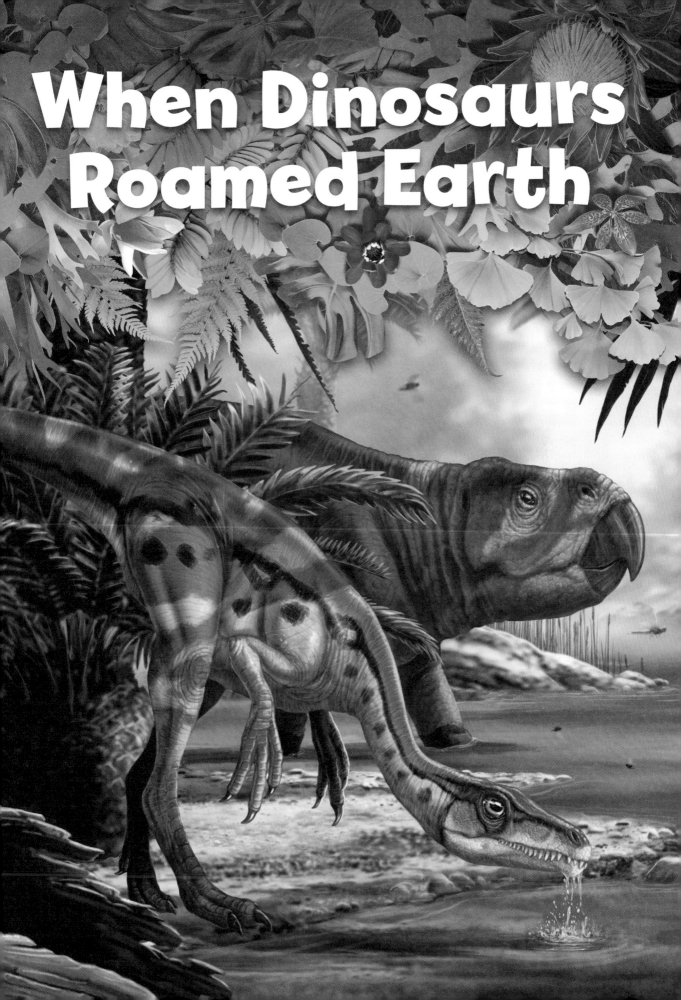

When Dinosaurs Roamed Earth

If **you look** at a map of Earth, you'll see water and seven main blocks of land. These blocks of land are called continents. Look closely and try to imagine pushing the continents together. They would almost fit into each other, like pieces of a puzzle! That's because over 250 million years ago, when the time of the dinosaurs began, they were connected. This huge area of land was called Pangaea (pan-JEE-uh).

There was
NO ICE near
the NORTH and
SOUTH POLES
during the time of
the dinosaurs.

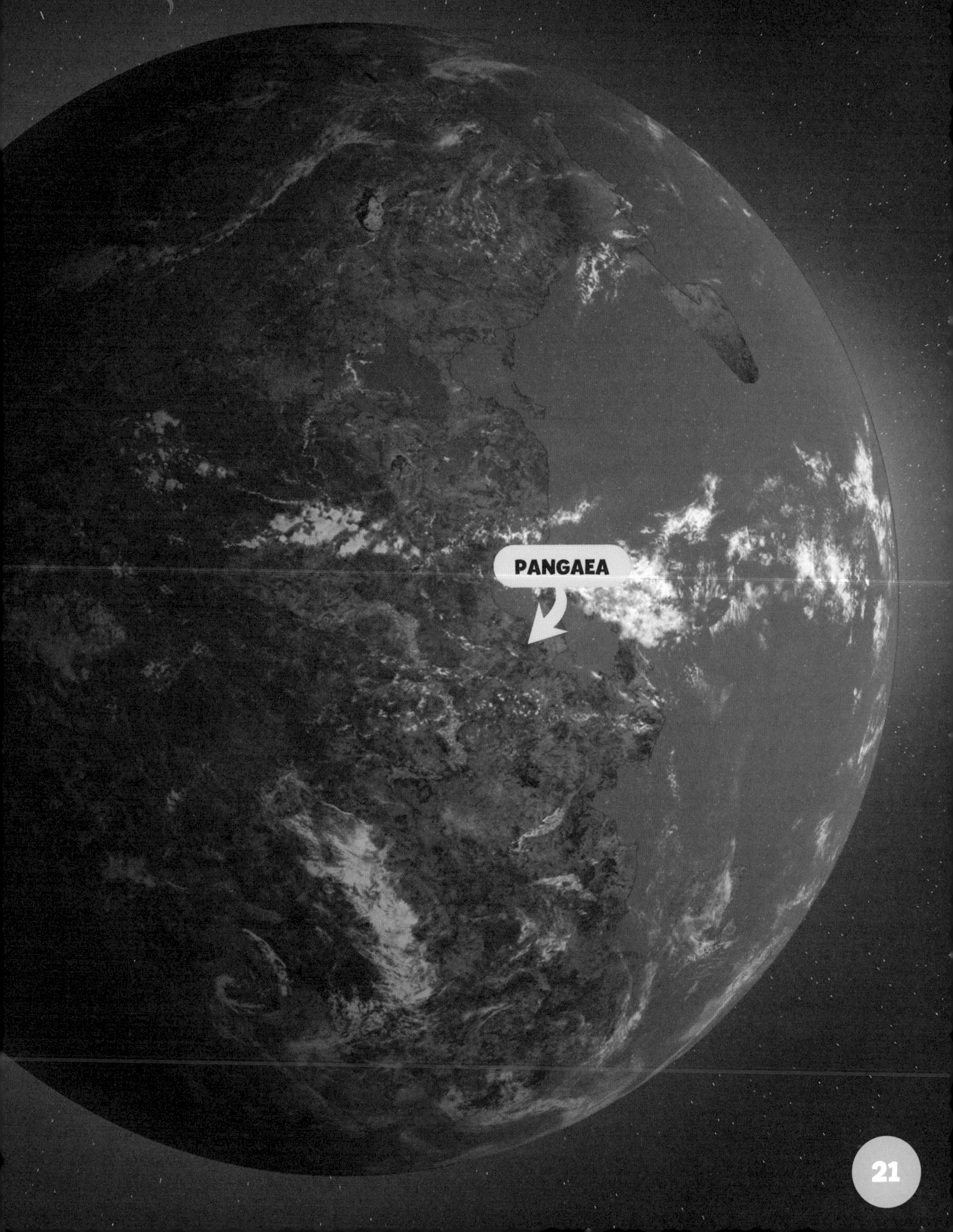
PANGAEA

Pangaea had volcanoes and deserts, and it was hot and dry. But over millions of years, the land began to stretch and pull apart. Some areas broke off and drifted slowly away from the mainland. The climate changed. Some areas cooled off. Other parts became damp and steamy, like the bathroom after a bath!

The damp areas looked like jungles. The land there was covered with lush, green plants and shrubs. Trees with needles, like pine trees, grew tall. After a while, palm trees appeared. Flowering plants bloomed. The flowers attracted bees and butterflies. These insects pollinated the plants. That helped more plants grow.

Prehistoric **DRAGONFLIES** had **WINGSPANS AS LONG AS** a **BASEBALL BAT.**

Flying insects weren't the only bugs in the neighborhood. Cockroaches scurried about. And small, rat-like mammals scrambled on the ground. Lizards crawled under bushes.

AN EARLY MAMMAL

The rest of Earth was water. Creatures of all sizes swam in the ocean. Tiny plants and animals called plankton floated on currents. Huge animals that looked like sea monsters ruled the seas. Some of these animals were marine reptiles called plesiosaurs (PLEEZ-ee-uh-sores). Plesiosaurs didn't have gills like fish do. Like humans, they had to hold their breath underwater.

Scientists think that **PLESIOSAURS TWISTED THEIR FLIPPERS** to help them swim.

All these animals lived during the Mesozoic (meh-zuh-ZO-ik) era, a time that spanned from 250 million to 66 million years ago. But one type of animal truly ruled the world during this time: the dinosaur.

What made DINOS different from other REPTILES? They all had legs that went straight under their bodies, not to the side.

NYASASAURUS

STEGOSAURUS

There were many types of dinosaurs. Some, like *Stegosaurus* (STEG-oh-SORE-us), walked on four legs. Others, like *Tyrannosaurus,* walked on two.

These reptiles lived on Earth for 165 million years. The age of dinosaurs is divided into three blocks of time: the Triassic (try-AS-ik), Jurassic (juh-RAH-sik), and Cretaceous (kruh-TAY-shuhs) periods. Not all types of dinosaurs lived at the same time.

The dog-size *Eoraptor* (EE-oh-RAP-tore) lived during the Triassic period. It was a fast runner. *Eoraptor* was an omnivore. It chowed down on both meat and plants.

The EARLIEST DINOSAURS walked on two legs.

BRACHIOSAURUS

The gigantic *Brachiosaurus* (BRACK-ee-oh-SORE-us) thundered around during the Jurassic period. It was a plant-eater, or herbivore. It had a long neck so it could eat the needles and leaves at the very top of tall trees. If four-story buildings existed back then, it could have eaten a plant off the roof.

It wasn't until the Cretaceous period that the famous carnivore, or meat-eater, *Tyrannosaurus rex* stomped about eating whatever it wanted!

Because the continents were once connected, and then separated, dinosaur bones have been found all over the world. One animal whose bones they won't find with dinosaur bones is humans! People were not yet alive during the age of dinosaurs.

Human ancestors didn't appear on Earth until between seven million and five million years ago. By then, all the land dinosaurs were gone.

PREHISTORIC HUMANS

Digging for Fossils

COLORADO, MONTANA, UTAH, and WYOMING are some of the BEST PLACES to find DINOSAUR BONES in the U.S.

It's hot in the desert.

A scientist wipes sweat from her fore-head. She puts her hand up to shield her eyes from the sun. She looks around, searching. There—in that rock. She sees something! It could be a small stone. Or could it be something else? She pulls out her hammer and chisel. She brushes away the dust. She digs, but carefully.

A PALEONTOLOGIST EXCAVATING A HADROSAUR FOSSIL

She loosens the dark material and lifts it to her tongue. Her tongue sticks to it. That means she has found a dinosaur bone!

The OLDEST FOSSILS found so far are about 3.45 BILLION years old.

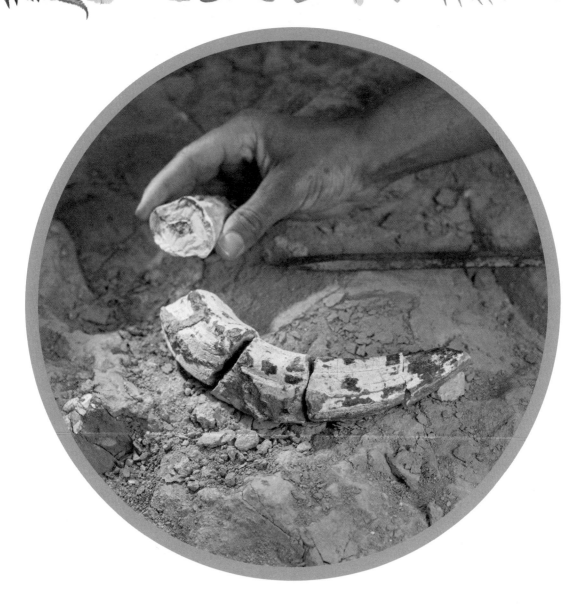

This scientist is a paleontologist (pay-lee-un-TALL-uh-jist). That's someone who studies the history of Earth through prehistoric fossils. Fossils are parts of plants and animals that have been preserved in rock. They can be leaves or bones or teeth.

After an animal dies, its bones remain. These bones may get buried under sand or mud. Sometimes minerals from the mud seep into tiny holes in the bones. Then, over many, many years, the bones and minerals harden, like cement. It doesn't happen often. But when the conditions are just right, a fossil is made.

A *T. REX* FOSSIL

The first COMPLETE DINOSAUR SKELETON was found IN 1858.

Scientists don't always know where to look for fossils, but they can guess. Some parts of Earth have more dinosaur bones than others. But fossils aren't just bones. They can be something the animal left behind, like footprints or even … poop!

Fossilized DINOSAUR POOP is called COPROLITE (KAH-pro-lite).

Found in France, one of **THE LONGEST** known strings of **DINOSAUR TRACKS** is 110 footprints.

Scientists, like detectives, follow dinosaur footprints. These footprints aren't just on the ground. They can appear on the side of tall rocks. Did dinosaurs walk up walls? No. But over millions of years, the ground on Earth shifted.

To help them **EAT MEAT**, most **CARNIVORES** had **SHARP TEETH.**

The paleontologist is excited about finding a bone. It may tell her a lot about the dinosaur. Based on the size of the bone, she can figure out how big a dinosaur was. And if she finds a tooth or fossilized poop, she will know what it ate. So she keeps digging.

Now she must carefully separate the thin layers of rock. Fossils are often sandwiched between layers of sedimentary rock. Sedimentary rocks are formed from tiny bits of larger rocks that are washed away. She doesn't want to damage any bones inside.

A DINOSAUR SPINE BURIED IN ROCK

45

Sometimes scientists find only a few bones. But sometimes they find almost an entire skeleton at once.

A PTEROSAUR SKELETON

This scientist has loosened several more fossils from the rock! She asks her team for help. Together, they dig for more bones. Then they wrap the bones in a plaster cast. It's a lot like what a doctor does for a broken arm. This keeps the fossil from breaking.

Sometimes scientists use **HELICOPTERS** to **MOVE FOSSILS.**

48

When they are finished, they will load up a truck with the wrapped-up bones. The fossils will travel to a storage room at a museum or university for testing. Eventually, scientists will x-ray, scan, and study the bones using computers. Then they can make three-dimensional models. These models show them how dinosaurs—and other prehistoric animals—behaved and grew.

No human has ever seen these ancient animals alive. And dinosaurs couldn't draw portraits or take selfies! But thanks to paleontologists, we know a lot about dinosaurs and what they looked like. There is still a lot to learn. Each year, paleontologists find about 50 new dinosaur species. One day, you could grow up to be a paleontologist, too!

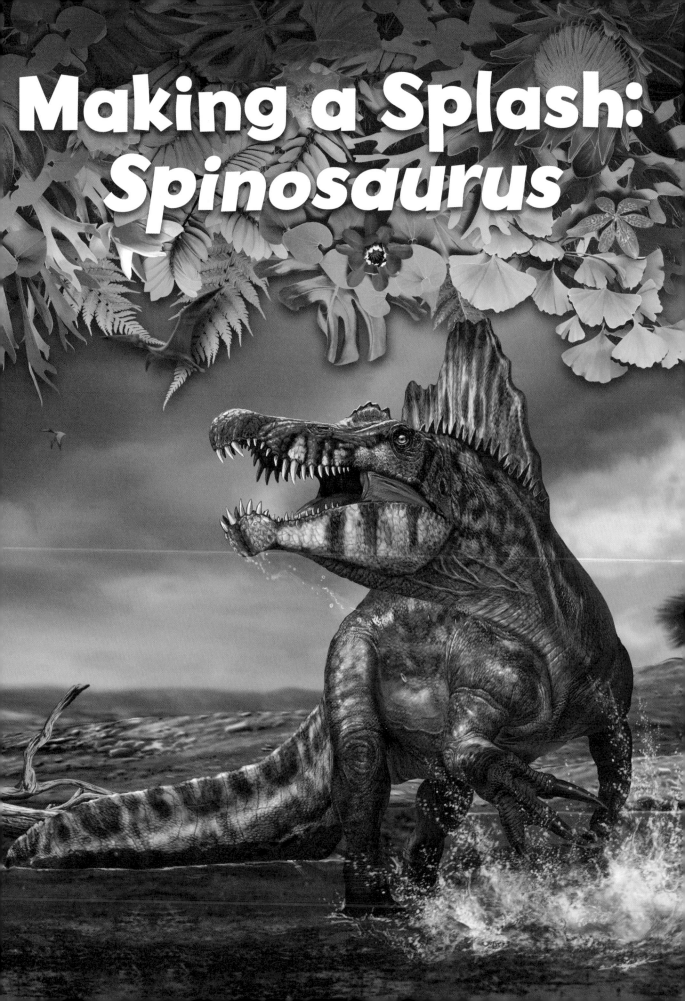

Making a Splash: *Spinosaurus*

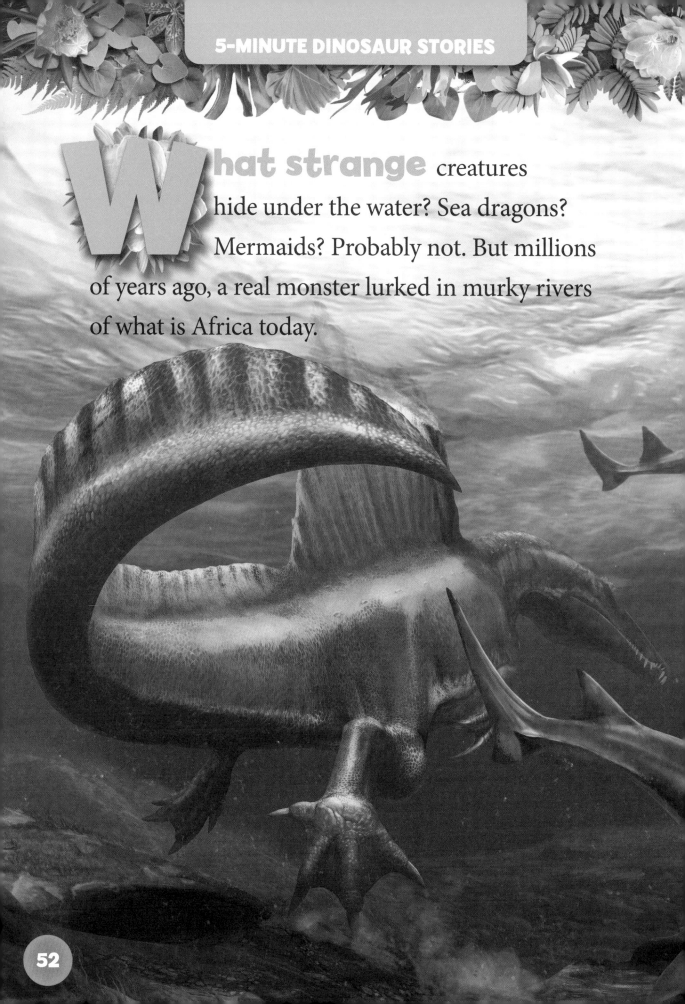

What strange creatures hide under the water? Sea dragons? Mermaids? Probably not. But millions of years ago, a real monster lurked in murky rivers of what is Africa today.

This monster watched carefully. If an ancient fish glided by, it would swim closer and closer. Then it would open its jaws, which were filled with six-inch (15-cm)-long teeth.

Chomp! This giant creature would catch its lunch.

SPINOSAURUS may have been the BIGGEST MEAT-EATER ever.

This dinosaur was enormous. It measured more than 50 feet (15 m) long. On its back, it had a giant fin. The fin looked like a sail. It was filled with long, bony spines. Sticking above the surface of the water, it would have been a scary sight. Animals spotting it would get the message: *Keep away!*

In 1912 a paleontologist found some bones from this creature in the desert in Egypt. He knew it was a dinosaur. And he knew it had some spines along its back. So he named it *Spinosaurus* (SPINE-oh-SORE-us).

THE SAHARA DESERT

He also found long, cone-shaped teeth, like crocodiles have. Cone-shaped teeth are good for catching fish. Millions of years ago, this desert was a maze of seas and rivers. The paleontologist guessed this dinosaur sometimes waded into the river looking for fish.

CROCODILES are not DINOSAURS— but the two are related.

Unfortunately, most of these fossils were destroyed during World War II. That made it hard for other paleontologists to learn new things about *Spinosaurus*. But in 2008, an amateur fossil hunter found new bones in the western part of the Sahara desert in Morocco. A young paleontologist, Nizar Ibrahim, recognized them: *Spinosaurus*.

Its SPINES made SPINOSAURUS'S SAIL stick up more than FIVE FEET (1.5 m) HIGH.

Nizar and his team returned to where the fossil hunter had found the bones. They began to dig in the red sands of the Sahara.

They uncovered bone after bone. The more they dug, the more bones they found. They even uncovered back bones with the spines attached. Nizar and the team also found some unusual tail bones. Those bones had spines as well.

NIZAR IBRAHIM

They shipped the bones back to the lab. With the help of other scientists, like Paul Sereno, Nizar put the bones together and studied them. The team learned some very interesting things. This animal had dense bones, which helped it stay underwater longer to hunt for food. And its nostrils were on top of its snout, near its eyes. It could breathe by sticking only a tiny bit of its head above the water.

SPINOSAURUS SKULL

Spinosaurus had short back legs and probably had webbed feet, like a duck's. These stumpy legs would have made it easier to walk along a muddy river bottom. And they helped the animal swim. Nizar and the others wondered if this dinosaur spent its time in the water.

So the team went back to the desert. And they found more *Spinosaurus* tail bones. Many dinosaurs had tails. But this tail looked like a fin. The animal could flap it from side to side, like a crocodile does. This motion would have pushed the dinosaur through the water. The team now had all the clues they needed.

CROCODILE TAIL

Scientists knew that non-dinosaur animals, like fish, lived in the water. And they knew that dinosaurs sometimes waded into the water—maybe even for a short swim. But now they had proof that at least one dinosaur spent a lot of its time in water. *Spinosaurus* was a real river monster after all.

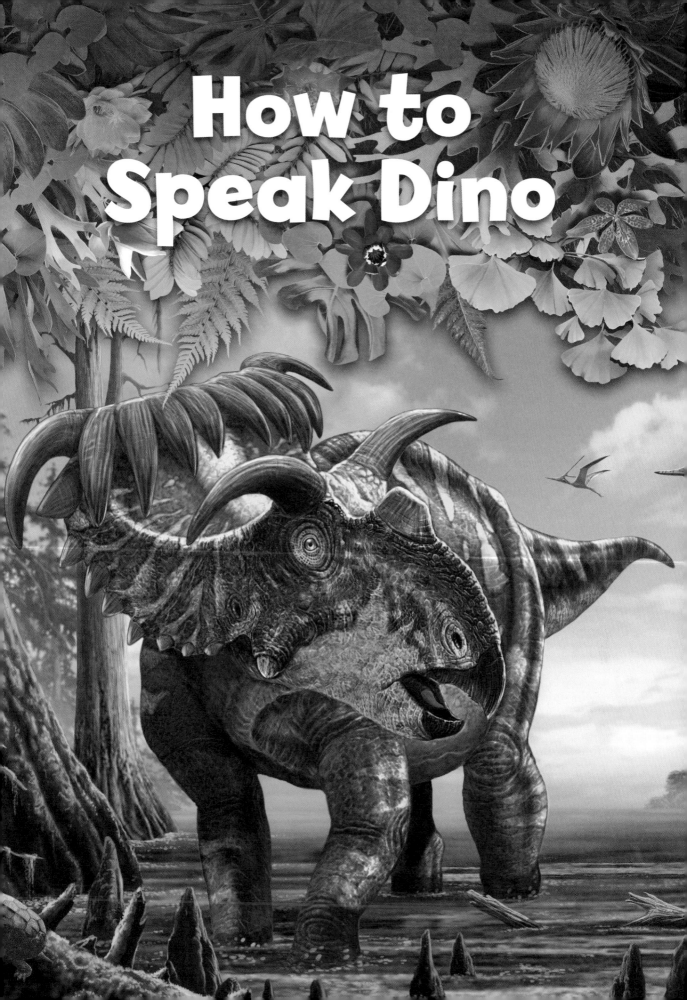

How to Speak Dino

Have you ever pictured a mighty *Tyrannosaurus rex* opening its tooth-filled mouth and giving a terrifying ROAR? Many people do. But *T. rex* didn't roar. Some scientists think it honked! It didn't sound like a goose. Because *T. rex* was so big, its honk would have sounded like an entire brass band playing at once!

GEESE send MESSAGES to each other by HONKING.

Dinosaurs probably couldn't roar. Roaring is a sound made by modern-day mammals like lions, tigers, and bears. These animals have large vocal cords in their necks that dinosaurs didn't have.

But dinosaurs weren't silent. They made all sorts of sounds. If you had lived during the age of dinosaurs, you would have heard booms and hisses. You might have heard trumpets, like elephants make. You would have even heard dovelike coos.

Dinosaurs, like birds, probably made **COOS** and **HOOTS** in their throats, with their **MOUTHS CLOSED.**

71

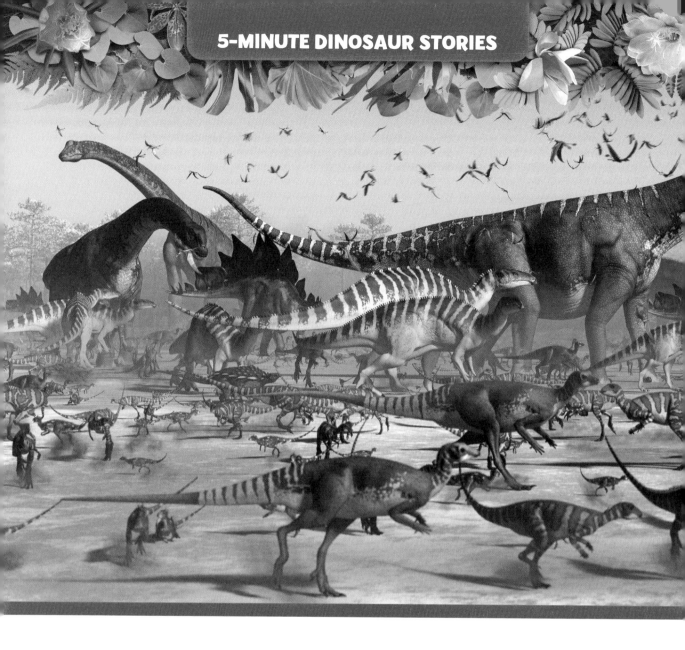

Not all people speak the same language. That was true for dinosaurs, too. Different species made different sounds. But while people can learn to speak other languages, dinosaurs couldn't. The sounds they produced depended on how their bodies were shaped.

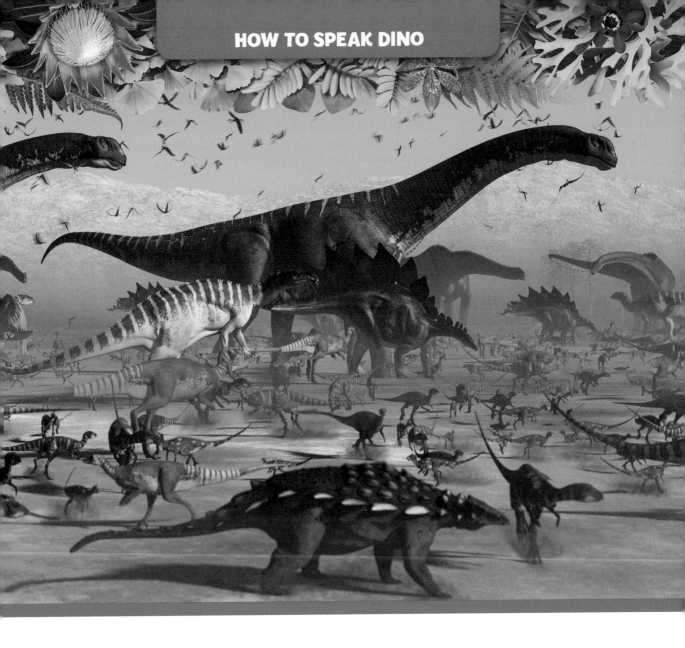

To understand what noises a dinosaur might have made, scientists look at the shape of the dinosaur's head and neck. Then they build models of the skulls and blow air through them. That tells them what noises a specific type of dinosaur could produce.

Dinosaur CRESTS worked a lot like the body of a MUSICAL INSTRUMENT to turn up the volume on their BOOMING CALLS.

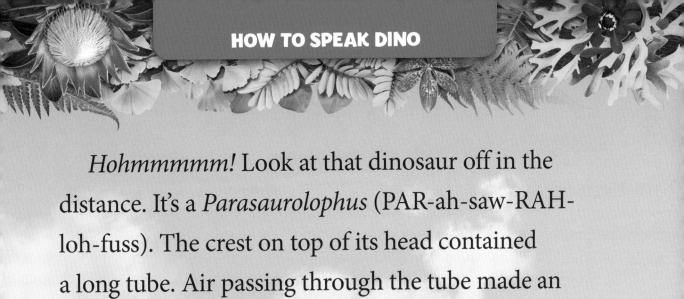

Hohmmmmm! Look at that dinosaur off in the distance. It's a *Parasaurolophus* (PAR-ah-saw-RAH-loh-fuss). The crest on top of its head contained a long tube. Air passing through the tube made an eerie sound like air being blown through a shell. The longer the tube, the deeper the sound.

Parasaurolophus was one of the loudest dinosaurs. What was it trying to say? Scientists are not sure. Maybe it was trying to scare away other dinosaurs. Or, it could have been looking for a mate, or calling to its herd. Or maybe all three!

DOGS CAN HEAR high-pitched whistles that **HUMANS CAN'T HEAR.**

To understand dinospeak, scientists also have to learn how dinosaurs *heard* sounds. Not all animals hear the same sounds. For example, elephants can hear one another's stomach rumbles from miles away. To communicate, dinosaurs of the same species had to be able to *hear* the sounds the others made.

Dinosaurs didn't have as many ear bones as humans. So they heard mostly low-frequency sounds. The skull shape of the *Sarmientosaurus* (SAR-mee-en-toe-SORE-us) allowed it to hear hums. These sounds carried well through the dense plants of the jungle.

Dinosaurs may have been able to hear really high-pitched squeaks, too. That helped parents hear the chirps of their babies.

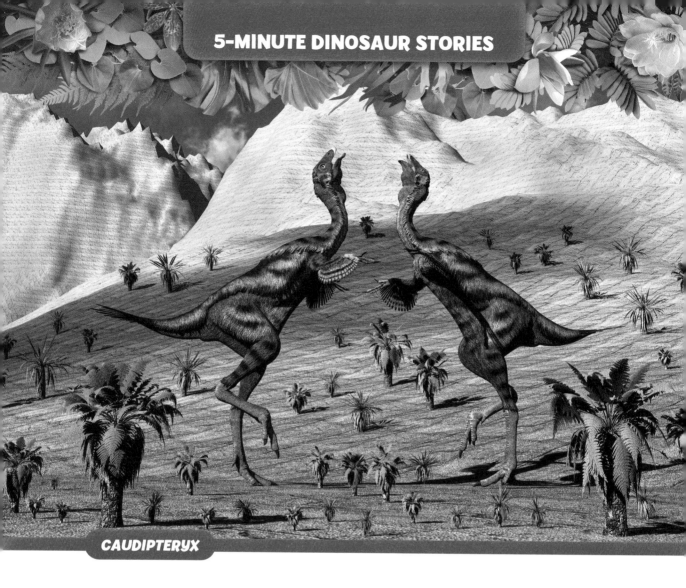

CAUDIPTERYX

Of course, dinosaurs had other ways to communicate. Like people, they spoke through body language. Fossil experts have found dinosaur scrape marks on rocks. These show that some dinosaurs moved their feet over and over in a pattern. Did this mean dinosaurs danced? It's possible. They may have hopped and bopped, like some birds do, to attract a mate.

Diplodocus (dih-PLOD-uh-kus) had a superlong tail—more than 45 feet (14 m). It may have used its tail to touch others of its kind—like people touch their friends. But scientists think it could also snap its tail. The whipcrack of this enormous tail could have been heard from far away.

The next time you go outside, listen! You might hear horns honking, doves cooing, and people saying "hello." Earth looks different today. The animals living on the planet are different, too. But just like in the time of the dinosaurs, it is still a place filled with sound.

MODERN-DAY DOVES

Apatosaurus:
Veggie Lover

It's late in the Jurassic period, in what is North America today. The forests are dark and full of plants and trees. *Thud, thud, thud.* A herd of *Apatosaurus* thunders by. It's hard to miss an *Apatosaurus*. This giant weighs more than five grown elephants and stands 15 feet (4.5 m) tall at the hip. That's almost as tall as three adult women.

BABY APATOSAURUS WEIGHED only about as much as a PET CAT, but grew very quickly!

A young *Apatosaurus* walks in between the adults. The herd hides it from one of the fiercest predators of all—*Allosaurus* (AL-oh-SORE-us). The young dinosaur stops to nibble some moss. It doesn't see the sneaky *Allosaurus* that is watching from behind a tree. A young *Apatosaurus* would be a tasty dinner for this meat-eater. But the large herd sees it and pushes the youngster along.

Together, the herd spends its days munching veggies. Lots and lots of veggies. The dinos stretch their long necks up to reach leaves on high branches. They swing their necks low to sweep up ferns along the ground.

Apatosaurus has to share food with other plant-eating dinosaurs. Luckily, different dinosaurs eat different plants from different levels in the forest. Some, like *Stegosaurus,* graze on low shrubs and moss. Others, like *Diplodocus,* rip leaves from the tallest trees.

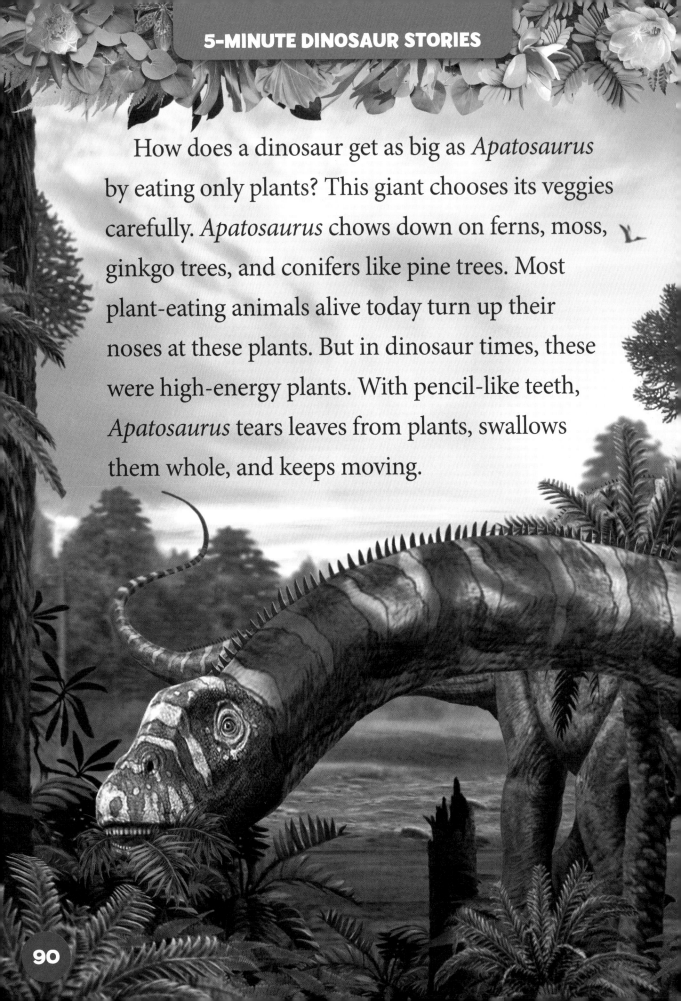

How does a dinosaur get as big as *Apatosaurus* by eating only plants? This giant chooses its veggies carefully. *Apatosaurus* chows down on ferns, moss, ginkgo trees, and conifers like pine trees. Most plant-eating animals alive today turn up their noses at these plants. But in dinosaur times, these were high-energy plants. With pencil-like teeth, *Apatosaurus* tears leaves from plants, swallows them whole, and keeps moving.

Apatosaurus LIVED to be 70 to 80 years old.

HADROSAURUS

Apatosaurus spent a lot of its day eating. But veggies can be hard to digest—even for dinosaurs. Some plant-eaters, like *Hadrosaurus,* had short teeth that could grind up plants. But not *Apatosaurus.*

Other dinosaurs, like *Barosaurus* (BAR-oh-SORE-us), had gastroliths. These were stones or pebbles that the animals swallowed. They churned food around like a mixer. But gastroliths haven't been found with *Apatosaurus* fossils, yet.

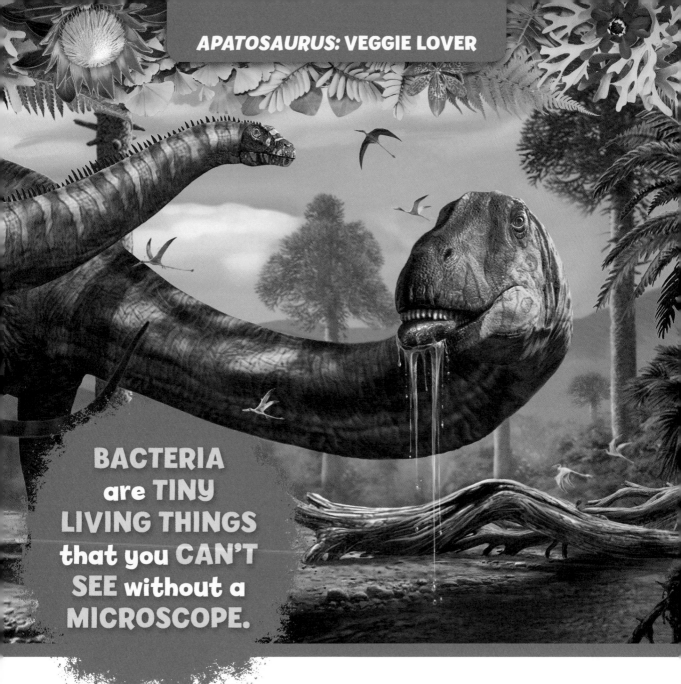

BACTERIA are TINY LIVING THINGS that you CAN'T SEE without a MICROSCOPE.

Is there another way *Apatosaurus* could have digested all those leaves? Scientists think that it had certain acids or tiny bacteria in its stomach that helped it break down its dinner. This bacteria would have also made *Apatasaurus* pass a lot of gas!

95

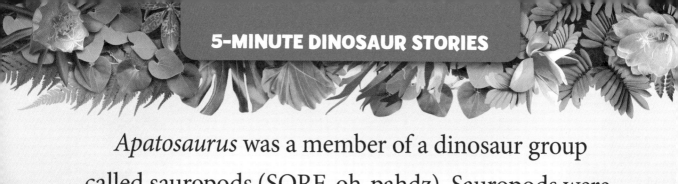

Apatosaurus was a member of a dinosaur group called sauropods (SORE-oh-pahdz). Sauropods were large dinosaurs with small heads and long necks. Their necks were up to 50 feet (15 m) long—six times longer than a giraffe's neck!

Some **SAUROPODS** ate about **1,000 POUNDS** (450 kg) of plants a day.

Apatosaurus's closest relative was *Brontosaurus* (brahn-tuh-SORE-uhs). They looked so much alike that at one time scientists thought *Apatosaurus* and *Brontosaurus* were the same animal! Some of *Apatosaurus*'s other relatives include *Brachiosaurus* and *Europasaurus* (yoo-ROPE-ah-SORE-us). *Europasaurus* was smaller and has been found only in modern-day Germany.

EUROPASAURUS

Brachiosaurus had **FRONT LEGS** that were **LONGER** than its **BACK LEGS** so it could reach leaves high in the trees.

With their long necks and little heads, sauropods may have looked a bit strange! But these gentle giants were built to last. Sauropods—like *Apatosaurus* and its relatives—strolled around Earth, munching and crunching, for more than 140 million years.

ONE OF *APATOSAURUS'S* SAUROPOD RELATIVES

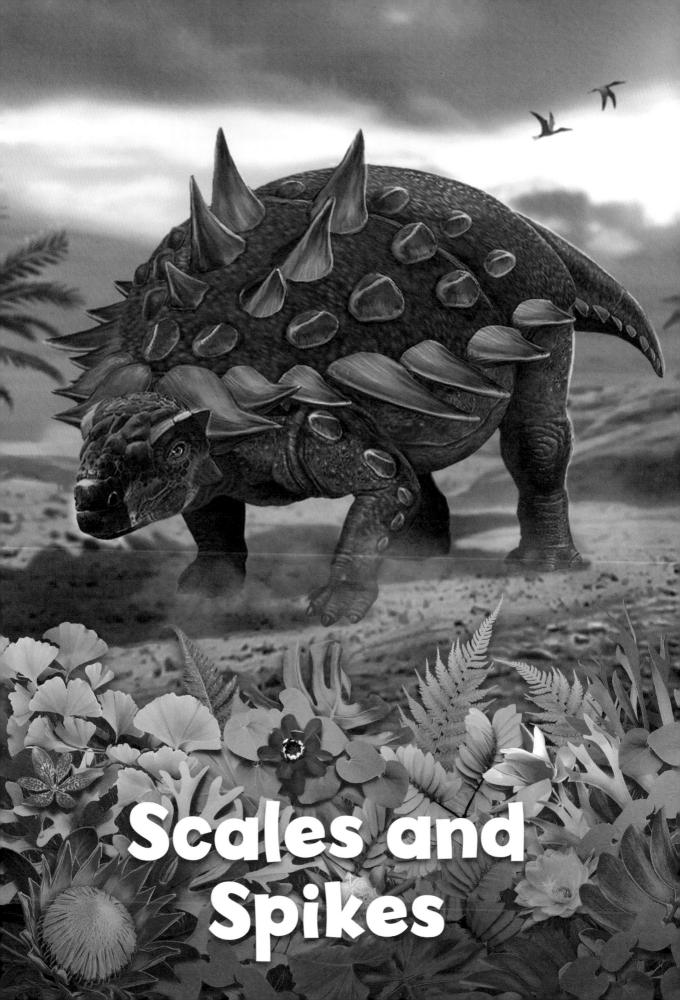

Scales and Spikes

Stegosaurus nibbles plants as it rambles along. It is a slow-moving dinosaur. Nearby, *Allosaurus* watches, hungry for a bite.

Carnotaurus (KAR-no-TORE-us) had ANGLED EYES that helped it JUDGE HOW FAR AWAY its prey was.

Meat-eaters like *Allosaurus* were predators. Some meat-eaters ate other dinosaurs. And they had body parts they used as weapons to help them attack. Many had very sharp teeth, like *Allosaurus*. Some, like *Tyrannosaurus*, had huge bodies.

ALLOSAURUS

To protect themselves against predators like *Allosaurus*, many plant-eaters had armor or spiky body parts. Some, like *Stegosaurus*, had bony plates sticking straight up on their backs. These may have warned other animals to stay away.

But *Allosaurus* was sneaky and strong. It hunted by surprising its prey. It stays hidden as *Stegosaurus* eats. Suddenly, *Allosaurus* races forward.

Stegosaurus has a powerful weapon: It swiftly swats *Allosaurus* away with its tail covered in long, sharp spikes. It can really hurt *Allosaurus*. Predators have to think twice about attacking an animal with such powerful armor.

And *Stegosaurus* wasn't the only dinosaur with armor and shields …

Ankylosaurus (AN-kye-loh-SORE-us) was covered in plates. The plates even protected its eyelids! *Ankylosaurus* looked like a military tank. It weighed around 10,000 pounds (4,500 kg). In addition to its armor, it had a not-so-secret weapon: a giant club at the end of its tail. One swing and *bam!* It could break the bones of its predators.

ANKYLOSAURUS STRIKING AN ANCIENT CROCODILE RELATIVE

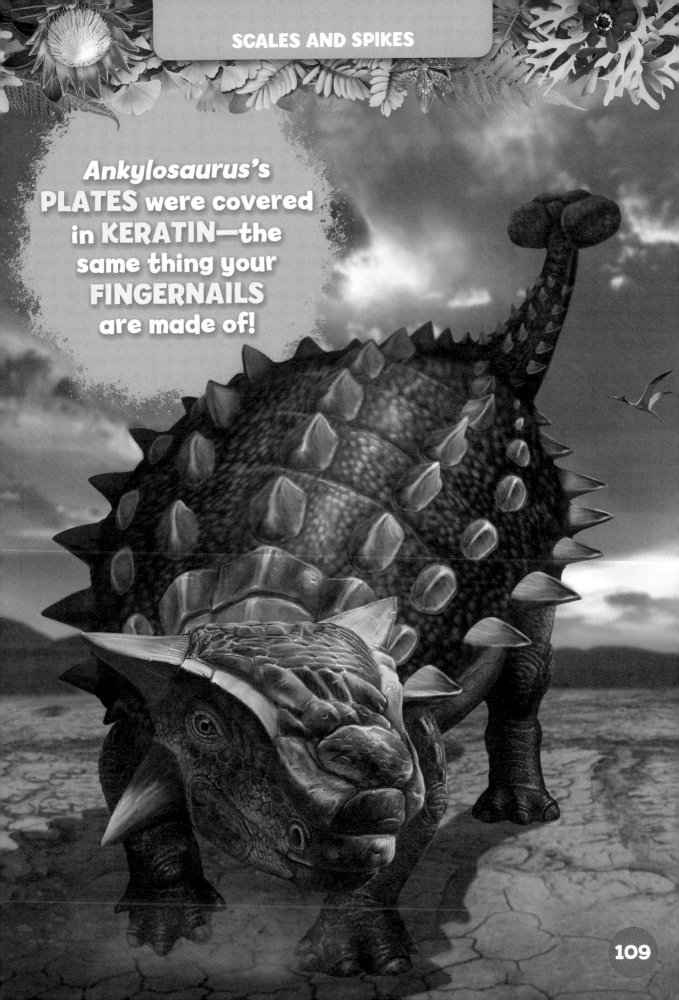

Ankylosaurus's PLATES were covered in KERATIN—the same thing your FINGERNAILS are made of!

BOREALOPELTA

ANKYLOSAURUS

Borealopelta's (BORE-ee-al-low-PEL-tuh) body was covered in large bony plates, too. It looked a lot like *Ankylosaurus*. But it had another protection—camouflage. Its light-colored belly blended in with the ground. From far away, it was hard to spot.

111

Triceratops (tri-SERR-uh-tops) had three horns on its gigantic head—two big ones on the top and a small horn on its nose. It also had a bony, ruffle-like frill on its neck. This armor helped it fight off predators.

But sometimes *Triceratops* fought other *Triceratops.* One might lower its head and thrust its horns forward. The other might push the horns aside, like a sword fighter responding to an attack. Scientists think two *Triceratops* might fight each other in battles over territory, food, or a mate— just as we see in some animals today.

Other dinosaurs wore their own helmets! *Pachycephalosaurus* (pack-ih-SEF-ah-low-SORE-us) had a nine-inch (23-cm) dome on the top of its head. The domed helmet was surrounded by spikes. It was protection against a hungry meat-eater. But scientists think this plant-eater may also have used its thick skull to headbutt other *Pachycephalosaurus*.

This dinosaur's NAME means "THICK-HEADED."

PACHYCEPHALOSAURUS

UTAHRAPTOR (BACK) AND *GASTONIA* (FRONT)

Maybe the best-protected dinosaur was *Gastonia* (gas-TONE-ee-ah). It had spikes like giant thorns on its neck, back, sides, and tail. It needed a lot of armor. *Gastonia* lived during the same time and in the same place as a large predator called *Utahraptor* (YOO-tah-RAP-tore).

As for the fanciest suit of armor, the best-dressed award goes to *Kosmoceratops* (COZ-mo-SERR-uh-tops). It had frills and horns and more knobs than you can count. But *Kosmoceratops* wasn't dressed for battle. All this decoration was probably meant to attract mates!

We still don't know for sure how dinosaurs used all their frills and spikes and armor. But we have a lot of clues from fossils. And we can see how animals today use their bodies. Some lizards and birds have dramatic frills. Mountain goats clash horns. But today's animal armor is probably nothing compared with the supersize stuff from the time of the dinosaurs.

Velociraptor at Night

Pretend you've traveled back in time to the age of dinosaurs. You are somewhere in what is Asia today. The sun is setting. That's when nocturnal animals wake up.

Something uncurls from sleep. It lifts its head off its back. It stands up on two feet. It's about the size of a wild turkey and comes up a little higher than a grown man's knee.

This creature has three forward-facing toes on its feet. At the end of its tail are long feathers. More feathers hang from its short arms. But this is no bird. It's *Velociraptor* (veh-LOSS-ih-RAP-tore).

Velociraptor was a type of dinosaur known as a theropod. Theropods walked on two feet. Other well-known theropods are *Spinosaurus* and *Tyrannosaurus*.

This *Velociraptor* is hungry. It's time to hunt.
Velociraptor heads out by itself.

It stalks along the dusty ground on two
strong legs.

Velociraptor's HABITAT was DRY LIKE A DESERT.

Velociraptor stops and sniffs the air. It has a very good sense of smell. Maybe it detects the fragrance of a frog or the smell of a small mammal.

No, it's a lizard! *Velociraptor* has spotted its dinner. With its sleek, narrow head, this dinosaur is built for speed. In a mighty burst, it chases its prey.

127

When *Velociraptor* gets close enough, it lowers its secret weapon—the claw. *Velociraptor* has a special long, curved claw on each of its feet. When it is ready to grab dinner, it uses this claw to stab the lizard and pin it down.

Velociraptor stuffs the lizard in its long, crocodile-like mouth. With its almost 60 knifelike teeth, it gobbles up its prey.

Velociraptor isn't a picky eater. Sometimes it finds leftover bones of a larger animal, like a pterosaur. It steals the bones and snacks on them. And sometimes *Velociraptor* picks a fight with an animal that is bigger or stronger.

Protoceratops wasn't much bigger than *Velociraptor*. It was only as tall as a kitchen counter-top. But at about 200 pounds (90 kg), it seriously outweighed *Velociraptor*. And it had strong jaws and a powerful bite. But *Velociraptor* could jump on top of the *Protoceratops.* Then it could dig its claw into the dinosaur's neck, behind its large bony frill, to take it down. Chances are *Velociraptor* would win.

What else is on the menu for *Velociraptor* tonight? It sniffs the air again. Maybe it is looking for dessert. And maybe it's time for you to travel back to the present day!

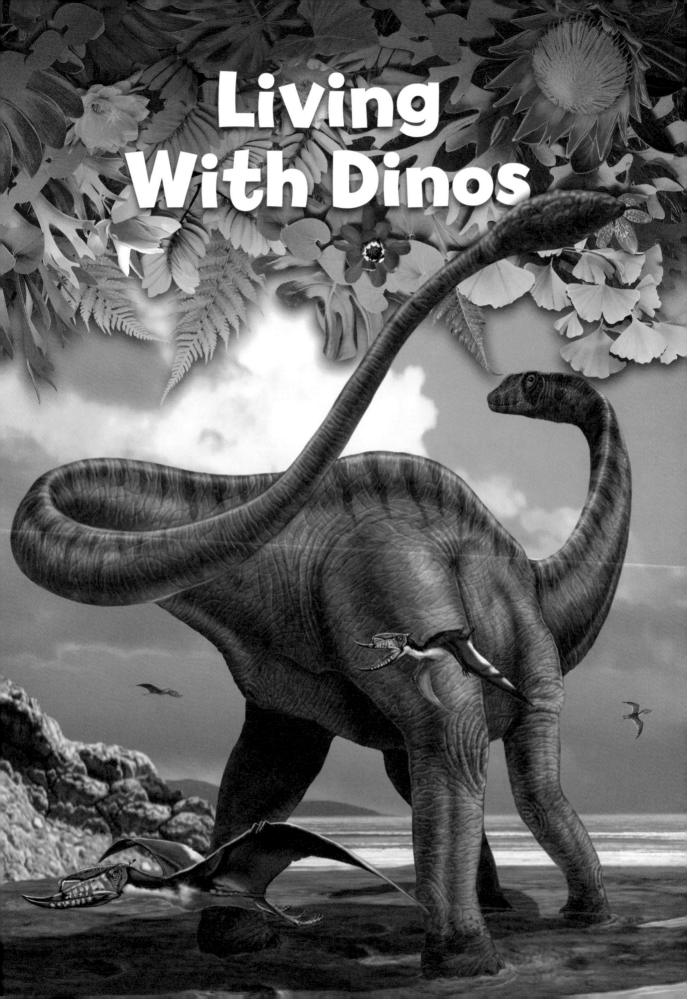

Living With Dinos

Humans didn't live during the time of the dinosaurs. But if we had, we would have seen a lot of other animals besides dinosaurs!

The **MESOZOIC ERA** lasted for hundreds of millions of years.

These animals all lived alongside the dinosaurs, but they may not have all lived at exactly the same time or place.

What would it be like to take a walk through the world in the time of dinosaurs?

If you looked up, you might notice a pterosaur (TEH-ruh-sore) circling in the sky. Pterosaurs weren't birds. They weren't dinosaurs. They were flying reptiles.

A pterosaur's wings were leathery. And they were attached to a superlong fourth finger. If a pterosaur spotted a small dinosaur below, it would swoop down and grab lunch.

If you stopped to smell a flower, you might hear something buzzing about. Ancient bees whizzed around flowering plants. They carried pollen and seeds from plant to plant, like bees still do today. One ancient bee was found with pollen on it. It was preserved in amber, or fossilized tree sap.

Just like modern bees help our plants grow,
ancient bees helped prehistoric plants grow.

If you went for a swim—watch out! Some sneaky, scary predators lived under the water, too. *Kaprosuchus* (ka-pro-SOO-kus), also known as the boar croc, glided close to the shore. Only its eyes would be visible above the surface of the water.

It might watch a plant-eating dinosaur munching a low shrub. The dinosaur wouldn't know it was in danger as the croc's feet dug into the mud by the shore. *Kaprosuchus* could then race out of the water and clamp its jaws around the dinosaur's neck.

The **BOAR CROC** was a **RELATIVE** of modern-day **CROCODILES.**

On the beach, you might see an animal with familiar-looking flippers. That would be *Archelon* (AAR-chuh-laan). This ancient turtle was a lot like some sea turtles living today. But compared with today's sea turtles, it was a giant. At about 13 feet (4 m) long, *Archelon* was the largest turtle that ever lived.

ARCHELON had a **LARGE, HOOKED BEAK.**

In the woods, you might spot two tiny eyes peeking out of the dark. And then you would see whiskers twitching on a pointy nose. This small creature was a *Morganucodon* (mor-gan-OO-coh-don). It looked like a rat with a longer face. It weighed only up to an ounce (28 g). It would have to scurry quickly to avoid the large feet of a herd of dinosaurs.

Despite its small size, it had a lot in common with humans. Like *Morganucodon,* we have hair, baby teeth followed by adult teeth, and jaws that can grind our food. *Morganucodon* was a mammal, like we are.

GINKGO TREES, illustrated below, existed DURING THE TIME OF THE DINOSAURS and are STILL AROUND TODAY.

If you were very lucky, you might glimpse another mammal. It had a bill like a duck. But it wasn't a duck. Its body was like a beaver's. But it wasn't a beaver. Meet the platypus! Relatives of the modern duck-billed platypus appeared on Earth during the Cretaceous period.

The **DUCK-BILLED PLATYPUS** lives in Australia.

The
ECHIDNA
is another
modern-day
MONOTREME.

The platypus is a special kind of mammal called a monotreme. Monotremes have hair like other mammals but lay eggs like reptiles. They have been on Earth for a very long time.

Dinosaurs ruled Earth for almost 165 million years. Small mammals, bees, cockroaches, lizards, sharks, horseshoe crabs, and snakes all shared space with the dinosaurs. Some became extinct. Some changed into modern-day animals. And some … survived! 🦖

T. rex: The Search for SUE

Sue Hendrickson always loved to find things. When she was a girl, she went looking for treasures in her neighborhood. She found lost coins. She found shells. Once she found a brass perfume bottle. When she was older, she joined diving teams and found sunken ships and sunken cities.

SUE (LEFT) WITH HER FAMILY

SUE EXPLORES AN OLD SHIPWRECK.

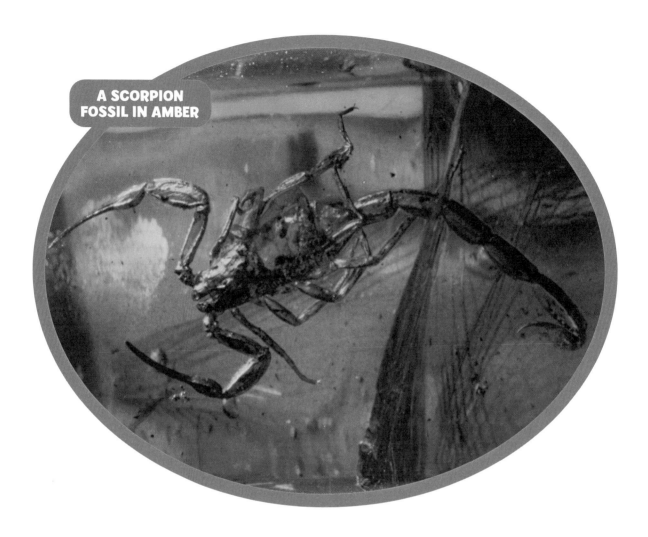

A SCORPION FOSSIL IN AMBER

Then Sue learned to find amber, or fossilized tree sap. She found ancient butterfly fossils in the amber. She taught herself about ancient insects. She taught herself about dinosaurs, too. She became a dinosaur hunter. And that's when she made her biggest find ever.

SUE AND HER TEAM EXCAVATE A FOSSILIZED WHALE.

On August 12, 1990, Sue was traveling with a group of paleontologists from the Black Hills Institute in South Dakota, U.S.A. On the last day of their dig, their truck got a flat tire. That gave Sue a chance to search a site she had spotted a couple of weeks before. While the others went to fix the tire, she hiked a few miles across the prairie and badlands. That's where she saw them—large, fossilized bones sticking out of the side of a cliff.

She hiked back to the rest of the team and asked them to take a look. The team dug for 17 days in burning hot sun. Using picks and shovels, they discovered bone after bone hidden in the sandstone. It turned out that they had found an almost complete fossilized dinosaur skeleton—of a *Tyrannosaurus rex*!

Tyrannosaurus rex means "tyrant lizard king." *T. rex* was a mighty dinosaur. Its sharp teeth were the size of bananas.

T. REX had TEENY-TINY ARMS compared to its body size.

Its jaws could crush a car. In the Cretaceous period, it stomped around what is now the western United States.

This carnivore had a sharp sense of smell and good eyesight that helped it find food. Luckily for prey, *T. rex* was not the speediest of the dinosaurs. But it wasn't slow, either. It could run at up to 12 miles an hour (19 km/h). That's fast enough to catch a human being!

T. REX may have sometimes HUNTED in PACKS.

THE *T. REX* BONES
SUE SPOTTED

The *T. rex* Sue Hendrickson found had lived a long life. A baby tyrannosaur would have been only about the size of a dog. But a fully grown *T. rex*, like the one Sue found, was 40 feet (12 m) long and could weigh up to eight tons (7.3 t).

The team covered each bone with a plaster bandage. The bandage was like a cast for a broken arm. Then they took them to the Black Hills Institute, where scientists spent many months carefully cleaning and sorting the bones. The team leader, Peter Larson, named the skeleton SUE, after the woman who discovered her.

Baby **T. REX** probably had **DOWNY FEATHERS,** like baby birds.

163

SUE'S SKULL is in its own case at the MUSEUM.

Many years later, scientists at the Field Museum in Chicago, Illinois, U.S.A., carefully cut open the plaster jackets that contained SUE the *T. rex.* They used delicate tools to clean the bones. With special glue, they filled any holes. Then they assembled the skeleton, sometimes making missing bones out of plastic. To mount the whole skeleton, they added metal rods to hold it up. Just mounting the *T. rex* took the workers eight months!

A SCIENTIST WORKS ON SOME OF SUE'S TEETH.

165

A MODEL SKULL SITS ATOP SUE'S SKELETON.

SUE was not the first *T. rex* ever found. But SUE is the most complete *T. rex* skeleton found so far.

SUE the *T. rex* has taught scientists many things about how dinosaurs survived and moved and how smart they were. She is so popular with visitors that she now lives in her very own room at the Field Museum. And Sue, the human? She kept on exploring new places and finding old things.

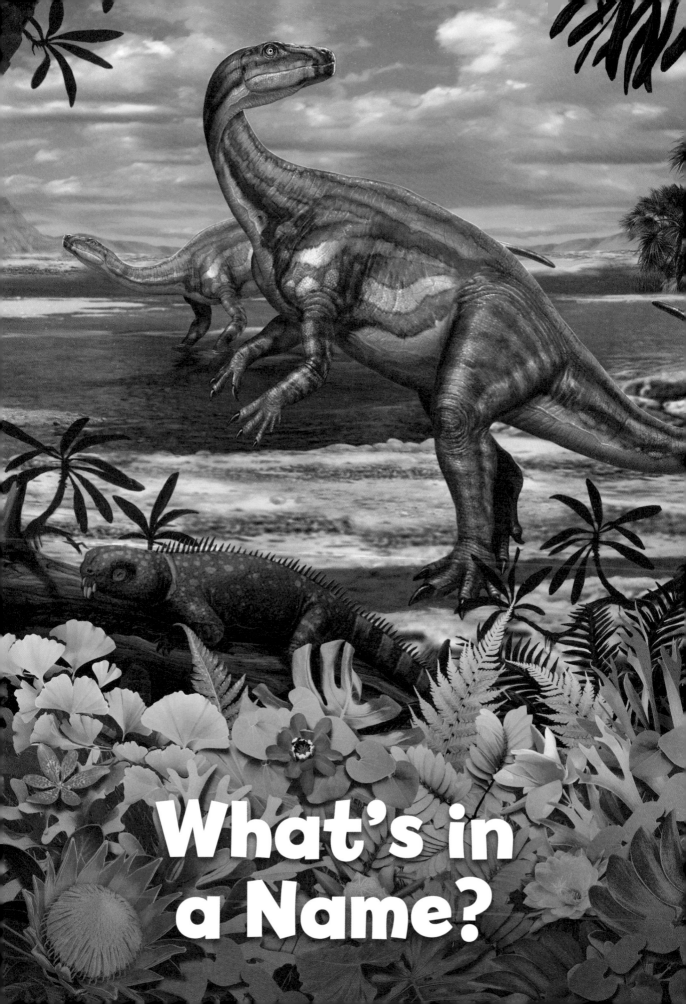

What's in a Name?

It's fun to name a new pet. Some people name their pet because of how it looks. Rusty is a good name for a red dog. Some pick a name because of how the animal acts. Squeaky is perfect for a noisy guinea pig.

But could you imagine naming an entirely new animal?

MEGALOSAURUS (meh-guh-loh-SORE-us) was the FIRST DINOSAUR to be NAMED by scientists.

A FOSSILIZED DINOSAUR JAW

In the 1800s, scientists were finding a lot of really big, old bones. But they didn't know what type of animal they came from. The bones looked like they came from giant lizards, so one scientist named the animal "fearfully great lizard." Like most scientists of the time, he looked to the Greek language, creating the word "dinosaur" by combining two Greek words.

173

For hundreds of years since then, people everywhere have been looking for dinosaur bones—and finding them! Over the years, scientists have found hundreds of different species of dinosaurs. That's a lot of dinosaurs to name!

When scientists find a new dinosaur, they pick the name. But how? Some scientists name dinosaurs after people. *Lambeosaurus* (LAM-bee-oh-SORE-us) was named in honor of Lawrence Lambe, who found some of its bones.

Some dinosaurs are named for how they look. *Yi qi* (EE chee) was discovered in China. Paleontologists think it had wings that were leathery, like a bat's. But they also had feathers along their top edge. In Mandarin Chinese, *Yi qi* means "strange wing."

Sometimes, dinosaurs are named based on the place they're from. The African country of Niger (nee-ZHAER) is in the heart of the dry, sandy Sahara. Several dinosaurs have been found there, but one didn't seem like any other known dinosaur.

This dinosaur looked pretty strange! It was an herbivore with a wide mouth like a shovel. It had thin teeth that ran straight across the front of its mouth. The dinosaur was named *Nigersaurus* (nee-ZHAER-SORE-us) after the place where it was discovered.

180

Sometimes scientists give dinosaurs funny names. In 2004, a dinosaur skull was discovered in South Dakota, U.S.A. Its spikes and horns reminded people of magical dragons from the Harry Potter series.

They named it *Dracorex hogwartsia* (DRAY-co-rex hog-WART-see-uh)—"dragon king of Hogwarts." But most scientists now think the skull belonged to a young *Pachycephalosaurus*.

181

Like Squeaky the guinea pig, some dinosaurs were named for their behavior. But in the case of *Oviraptor* (OH-vih-RAP-tore), it was named after something it never did!

Oviraptor HAD NO TEETH.

When *Oviraptor* was first discovered, its skull was found with some dinosaur eggs. Scientists thought the eggs were from a plant-eating dinosaur. That meant that *Oviraptor,* a carnivore, was stealing them. So the dinosaur was named *Oviraptor,* which is Greek for "egg thief." Later, however, paleontologists returned to the area. They discovered more eggs. These eggs, they realized, were baby *Oviraptor.* *Oviraptor* was protecting its babies. It wasn't an "egg thief" after all!

If you find a dinosaur fossil in your own backyard in the United States, you can keep it. And if it happens to be a new type of dinosaur, you might just get to name it.

What name would you choose?

Fluff Those Feathers

SEAGULL

If you stand outside

for even a little while, you'll probably see something with feathers flit by. You know what it is: a bird. All modern birds have feathers. Ancient birds had feathers, too. But they weren't the only animals to strut some fluff. Some dinosaurs also had feathery plumes.

Psittacosaurus (SIT-ah-co-SORE-us) had a face that looked like a parrot and feather-like bristles sticking straight up on its tail. Was *Psittacosaurus* a bird? No, it was a dinosaur.

Caihong juji (KYE-hung JUH-jee) had fluffier feathers. They were rainbow-colored. And they changed color in different light, like some humming-birds' feathers do. But *Caihong juji* was a dinosaur, not a bird.

Velociraptor wasn't a bird either. But in fossils, its arms have little bumps—called quill bumps—where feathers would have been. Before *Velociraptor* became a fossil, it had arms covered with long feathers.

Not all dinosaurs had them, but feathers were useful for the ones that did. Some used their feathers for warmth or to keep their eggs warm. Others may have used them for camouflage, or for decoration. But dinosaurs were definitely *not* birds, and their bodies and feathers were not made for flying … right? Things weren't always that simple.

This dinosaur's name means "ANCIENT WING."

Archaeopteryx (ARK-ee-OP-turr-icks) lived 150 million years ago. It was a meat-eating dinosaur with sharp teeth and a long, bony tail. Scientists are pretty sure that this animal could fly, or at least glide, in the air. They think this dinosaur might be the ancestor of all birds.

In the 1990s, fossil hunters found dinosaur bones in Antarctica. These bones belonged to *Vegavis* (VAY-guh-viss). It lived at the end of the dinosaur age. *Vegavis* looked a lot like a duck. It may even have quacked like a duck! And … it flew like one. But it was a dinosaur. Right? Or was it a duck?

DROMAEOSAUR CHASING *VEGAVIS*

When scientists took a closer look at its skeleton, they found that *Vegavis* had a lot in common with the skeletons of dinosaurs and of modern birds. It turns out that *Vegavis* was both: bird and dinosaur!

MALLARD

Ancient birds—like *Vegavis*—were actually dinosaurs all along. Scientists call them "avian dinosaurs." Today, we know that all birds are really modern-day dinosaurs.

Sixty-six million years ago, land dinosaurs vanished, or became extinct. Most scientists think this extinction was caused mainly by a giant asteroid.

The CRATER from the ASTEROID is still on Earth today, PARTLY BURIED UNDERWATER.

The asteroid crashed into Earth in what is Mexico today. It sparked earthquakes and floods. It made the climate very hot. Land dinosaurs—like *Ankylosaurus, Triceratops,* and *T. rex*—could not survive.

NOT ALL DINOSAURS were BIRDS, BUT ALL BIRDS are DINOSAURS.

HORNBILL

But the avian dinosaurs—also known as birds— lived. They were small and needed less food than the land dinosaurs. They could travel farther faster by flying. That allowed them to escape some of the effects of the asteroid.

201

The avian dinosaurs that survived extinction changed over time. They lost their teeth and bony tails. They branched off into more than 10,000 different species like pelicans, parrots, and raptors. They became modern-day birds.

PELICANS

BLUE JAY

ARCHAEOPTERYX

So look outside your window. The next time you see a bird fly by, remember that you are looking at a small, feathered dinosaur! 🦖

Glossary

Ancestor: a family member that lived a long time ago, like a great-great-grandparent

Asteroid: a piece of rock or metal from space that burns through Earth's atmosphere and hits the ground

Avian: relating to birds

Bacteria: microscopic single-celled living things

Camouflage: natural coloring or marking that allows animals or objects to hide by making them look like their surroundings

Carnivore: a meat-eater

Conifer: a group of many kinds of evergreen trees that do not lose their leaves in the fall

Continent: one of seven large land divisions on Earth: North America, South America, Europe, Asia, Africa, Australia, and Antarctica

Coprolite: fossilized feces or poop

Crest: a grouping of feathers, fur, or skin on the top of an animal's head

Cretaceous: the third and last period of the Mesozoic era, 145 million to 66 million years ago

Extinct: no longer existing

Fossil: a preserved part or trace of an ancient animal or plant

Frill: a feature around the neck of an animal that was, in the case of dinosaurs, made of either bone or cartilage

Gastrolith: a stone, sometimes called a gizzard, that helps grind food in the stomach

Genes: parts of the biological material that are passed down from parent to child

Herbivore: a plant-eater

Jurassic: the period of time from 201 million to 145 million years ago

Keratin: the bony sheath that makes up some dinosaur horns and covers their claws, found also in human fingernails

Mammal: a group of animals, including humans, that have backbones, breathe air, have hair, and drink their mother's milk

Mesozoic: the era of geologic time that includes the Triassic, Jurassic, and Cretaceous periods when dinosaurs lived on Earth

Nocturnal: active during the night

Omnivore: a living thing that eats both meat and plants

Paleontologist: a scientist who studies the history of Earth through fossils (sometimes of dinosaurs)

Plankton: tiny animals and plants that drift or float in oceans and lakes

Pollinate: to carry pollen from one plant to another to produce seeds

Predator: an animal that hunts other animals (prey) for food

Preserve: to protect something in its original state

Prey: an animal that a predator hunts and kills for food

Primate: a member of a group of animals that includes monkeys, apes, and humans

Reptile: a group of animals, including lizards and snakes, that have backbones and scaly skin and lay eggs

Sauropod: a large four-legged plant-eating dinosaur with a long neck and tail

Sedimentary: a rock that is formed when many small pieces of other rock are joined together

Skeleton: a stiff structure, made mainly of bone, that supports the body's soft tissues and organs

Species: a category, or kind, of animal or plant

Triassic: the period of time from 252 million to 201 million years ago

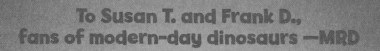

To Susan T. and Frank D.,
fans of modern-day dinosaurs —MRD

Copyright © 2024 National Geographic Partners, LLC

All rights reserved. Reproduction of the whole or any part of the contents without written permission from the publisher is prohibited.

NATIONAL GEOGRAPHIC and Yellow Border Design are trademarks of the National Geographic Society, used under license.

Since 1888, the National Geographic Society has funded more than 14,000 research, conservation, education, and storytelling projects around the world. National Geographic Partners distributes a portion of the funds it receives from your purchase to National Geographic Society to support programs including the conservation of animals and their habitats. To learn more, visit natgeo.com/info.

For more information, visit nationalgeographic.com, call 1-877-873-6846, or write to the following address:

National Geographic Partners, LLC
1145 17th Street NW
Washington, DC 20036-4688 U.S.A.

More for kids from National Geographic: natgeokids.com

National Geographic Kids magazine inspires children to explore their world with fun yet educational articles on animals, science, nature, and more. Using fresh storytelling and amazing photography, *Nat Geo Kids* shows kids ages 6 to 14 the fascinating truth about the world—and why they should care. natgeo.com/subscribe

For rights or permissions inquiries, please contact National Geographic Books Subsidiary Rights: bookrights@natgeo.com

Designed by Brett Challos

Hardcover ISBN: 978-1-4263-7648-1

ACKNOWLEDGMENTS

The publisher would like to thank Steve Brusatte for his expert review and Sue Hendrickson for sharing her story and photographs. The publisher would also like to thank the book team: Kathryn Williams, project editor; Lori Epstein, photo manager; Sarah Gardner, associate photo editor; Katherine Kling, fact-checker; Alix Inchausti, senior production editor; and Lauren Sciortino and David Marvin, associate designers.

Printed in China
24/LPC/1

PHOTO CREDITS

Illustrations by Franco Tempesta/© National Geographic Partners, LLC, unless otherwise noted below.
AD=Adobe Stock; NGIC=National Geographic Image Collection; SS=Shutterstock
Front Cover: (palm trees), estevez/SS; (leaves and flowers), Jeffrey Mangiat/Mendola Ltd; (volcano), Alena Stalmashonak/SS; (shadow), foxie/SS; (yellow paper texture), YamabikaY/SS; **Spine:** OlgaChernyak/SS; **Back Cover:** (palm trees), estevez/SS; (leaves and flowers), Jeffrey Mangiat/Mendola Ltd; (yellow paper texture), YamabikaY/SS; **Interior:** (leaves and flowers throughout), Jeffrey Mangiat/Mendola Ltd; 1 (palm trees), estevez/SS; 1 (yellow paper texture), YamabikaY/SS; 1 (volcano), Alena Stalmashonak/SS; 4-5, Daniel Eskridge/Alamy Stock Photo; 6, Stocktrek Images, Inc./Alamy Stock Photo; 7, The Natural History Museum, London/Science Source; 8, Juergen Freund/Nature Picture Library; 9, ©Zhao Chuang/PNSO; 12, James Kuether/Science Source; 14-15 (UP), Catmando/SS; 14-15 (LO), Rawpixel/SS; 18, Sinclair Stammers/Science Source; 20-21, ManuMata/SS; 26-27, Daniel Eskridge/AD; 35, paleontologist natural/SS; 36, Francois Gohier/Science Source; 37, Francois Gohier/Science Source; 38, Gorodenkoff/AD; 39, Paolo Verzone/NGIC; 40-41, The Natural History Museum/Alamy Stock Photo; 42, Breck P. Kent/SS; 43, Nataliya/AD; 44, Mike Hettwer/NGIC; 45, Jaahnlieb/Dreamstime; 46, Akkharat Jarusilawong/SS; 47, Philippe Psaila/Science Source; 48, Erik Tunstad; 49, Paolo Verzone/NGIC; 52-53, Davide Bonadonna/NGIC; 57, cceliaphoto/AD; 58, Kat Keene Hogue/NGIC; 59, Mike Hettwer/NGIC; 60, Mike Hettwer/NGIC; 61, Kat Keene Hogue/NGIC; 62, Klaus Steinkamp/Alamy Stock Photo; 63, Paolo Verzone/NGIC; 64, Kritsada Promyim/SS; 68, Nigel/AD; 70-71, Dotted Yeti/SS; 72-73, James Kuether/Science Source; 74-75, Daniel Eskridge/AD; 76, Mary Swift/AD; 80, MasPix/Alamy Stock Photo; 82, oioioio/AD; 110, Julius Csotonyi/Royal Tyrrell Museum; 114, Daniel Eskridge/AD; 136-137, Catmando/SS; 139, Warpaint/SS; 140, The Natural History Museum, London/Science Source; 141, Andy Sands/Nature Picture Library; 142-143, MR1805/Getty Images; 144-145, Michael Rosskothen/AD; 148, Doug Gimesy/Nature Picture Library; 149, pelooyen/AD; 151-155, Sue Hendrickson; 156-163, © 2024 Black Hills Institute of Geological Research, Inc.; 164, schusterbauer/AD; 165, NGIC; 166-167, Field Museum of Natural History; 168, Sue Hendrickson; 173, The Natural History Museum/Alamy Stock Photo; 178-179, Kostyantyn Ivanyshen/Stocktrek Images/Getty Images; 181, Phil Wilson/Stocktrek Images/Science Source; 183, Daniel Eskridge/AD; 184, piyaphunjun/AD; 186, Sergii Figurnyi/AD; 189, Velizar Simeonovski/Field Museum of Natural History; 195, Monica Serrano/NGIC; 196, Donald M. Jones/Minden Pictures; 197, Nicholle R. Fuller/Science Source; 200, Phillip Krzeminski; 201, Staffan Widstrand/Wild Wonders of China/Nature Picture Library; 202-203, Guy Edwardes/Nature Picture Library; 204, steheap/AD; 205, dottedyeti/AD